PEN & BRUSH LETTERING & ALPHABETS

50 Alphabets
arranged in eight sections
for students & designers

FIFTEENTH EDITION

BLANDFORD PRESS

Poole   Dorset

FIRST PUBLISHED IN THE UK, 1929

FOURTEENTH EDITION, 1967

FIFTEENTH EDITION, 1970

REPRINTED 1973

REPRINTED 1976

REPRINTED 1979

Copyright© 1960, 1967, 1970, Blandford Press Ltd.

Link House, West Street,
Poole, Dorset, BH15 1LL

ISBN 0 7137 0187 0

Reproduced printed and bound in Great Britain
at The Pitman Press, Bath

CONTENTS

INTRODUCTION

THE lettering which we use to-day has been handed down from early times. In fact it has been used for more than two thousand years, for our present main upright alphabet, whatever variety of "face" it may have, was derived from the Romans and is known as "Roman." We may distort this lettering, we may vary it, we may modernize it or do what we will, but always we come back with a sigh of relief to the pure Roman. It has a serenity, repose, a simplicity and above all a clarity which make it one of the greatest symbols of civilization. The small letters or miniscules, in printer's terms "lower case," have been evolved with the demand for flowing speed and there is no classic reference such as the Trajan inscription as in the upper case.

The following pages contain a selection of alphabets which act as a reference to the student, designer, or the professional sign and showcard writer and commercial artist. It is because of the variety of lettering which is in use to-day that there is need for such a book as this, which has now gone into fifteen impressions and has become a standard reference book.

In modern practice, lettering has become part of a power of publicity and propaganda. So much depends on lettering to convey the meaning, the emotion, or even the atmosphere, that it has become a work which at all times calls for thought, skill, and originality.

Lettering is like the voice of the elocutionist. It can portray joy and melancholia, it can shout or whisper, it can be loud and blatant or soft and refined, it can strike a note of urgency or of restraint; and these are the qualities which the modern advertiser and user of lettering wishes to employ. The alphabets shown are designed for use on a great variety of occasions. How and when is, of course, at the discretion of the letterer. The Roman carries dignity, the heavy grotesque letter clamours for attention, script may denote urgency. Each alphabet expresses something different.

It is necessary to mention that numerous types of lettering on one design or card cause confusion and decrease legibility and are consequently to be avoided. It is best that styles should be related, using for example upper case for headlines and lower case for body matter, and perhaps italics or script for something which should be outstanding. It is interesting to see how a firm can build up its own individuality in advertising by always using the same type of lettering. An advertiser is often recognized by the style of lettering in his announcements before the name is glanced at.

The alphabets in this book have been divided broadly into sections:—The Serif, Italics, Sans Serif, Shadow, Script, Numerals, Unusual Styles. Where samples of type are shown, these have mostly been selected from the "MONOTYPE" range.

It is impossible to cover every particular type of lettering that has existed or does exist, but basic alphabets in general use to-day are included, and numerous examples of how they can be adapted. From these the artist will find sufficient material to exercise his creative imagination.

ABCDEFGI HJKLMNO PQRSTUV WXYZ

PERPETUA LIGHT TITLING which has the matchless proportions of the classical Roman letter.

abcdefghij klmnopqr stuvwxyz

PERPETUA—Roman lower case.

ABCDEFGH IJKLMNOP QRSTUVW XYZ

abcdefghijklm nopqrstuvwxyz

BODONI—A much used modern style Roman in which strength is combined with delicacy because of the contrasting heavy descenders and fine ascenders.

ABCDEFGH
IJKLMNOP
QRSTUVW
XYZ

abcdefghijk
lmnopqrstu
vwxyz

ULTRA BODONI—This striking, heavy letter gives an effect of weight and boldness.

ABCDEFGHIJ KLMNOPQR STUVWXYZ

abcdefghij klmnopqr stuvwxyz

BEMBO—One of the loveliest of all old-face designs.

ABCDEFGH
IJKLMNO
PQRSTUV
WXYZ

abcdefgh
ijklmnopq
rstuvwxyz

TIMES BOLD—A twentieth-century contribution to type design.

ABCDEFGHIJ
KLMNOPQRS
TUVWXYZ

abcdefghij
klmnopqrs
tuvwxyz

SLIM BLACK—A condensed letter of distinction.

ABCDEFGHJ
KLMNOPQR
STUVWXYZ

abcdefghijkln
mopqrstuw
vxyz

MONARCH—A pen-lettered alphabet combining strength with dignity.
Its characteristic serifs can best be put in finally with the brush.

A B C D E F G H I J
K L M N O P Q R
S T U V W X Y Z

a b c d e f g h i j k l m
n o p q r s t u v w x y z

ROCKWELL—An even thickness letter with slab serifs.

ABCDEFGHIJ
KLMNOPQR
STVUWXYZ

abcdefghijklm
nopqrstuvwxyz

PERPETUA—The italic form of the alphabet on page 7.   Note the
slight modification in the proportion of letters and the elliptical curves.

ABCDE
FGHIJK
LMNOP
QRSTU
VWXYZ

A single-stroke broad-nib alphabet of classical proportions. A good example
of fine penmanship of a style used in formal work.

a b c d e f

g h i j k l

m n o p q

r s t u v

w x y z

ABCDEFGH
IJKLMNOP
QRSTUVW
XYZ

abcdefghijklmn
opqrstuvwxyz

GILL BOLD SANS SERIF ITALIC

ABCDEFG
HIJKLMN
OPQRSTU
VWXYZ

abcdefghij
klmnopqr
stuvwxyz

TIMES BOLD ITALIC—the italic version of the alphabet shown on page 11.

ABCDEFGHIJ KLMNOPQRS TUVWXYZ&

abcdefghijklmno pqrstuvwxyz

1234567890

GOUDY BOLD ITALIC—An attractive, legible letter, which has more
strength than most of the italic faces.

ABCDEFG
HIJKLMN
OPQRSTU
VWXYZ

abcdefghijklm
nopqrstuvwxyz
1234567890

A single-stroke pen alphabet. This is particularly suitable for rapid show-card and price ticket work, as its very essence is simplicity. For this page a Myers No. 1 broad nib was used.

ABCDEFG
HIJKLMN
OPQRSTU
VWXYZ

abcdefghi
jklmnopqr
stuvwxyz

1234567890

A slightly expanded italic sans-serif letter, based on FTF's 'Washington' design, which is becoming increasingly popular. For best effect it should be used sparingly, and with plenty of white space.

ABCDEF GHIJKL MNOPQ RSTUVW XYZ

abcdefghijklmn
opqrstuvwxyz

GILL SANS TITLING—A legible, pleasant and very readable face. Suitable for headings where copy is short, but if used to any great extent the effect is monotonous. Gill Sans lower case is shown in the frame.

A B C D E
F G H I J K
L M N O P
Q R S T U
V W X Y Z

GILL SANS BOLD TITLING—gives weight.

ABCDEFG
HIJKLMN
OPQRSTU
VWXYZ

abcdefghij
klmnopqr
stuvwxyz

GILL SANS **EXTRA BOLD** gives emphasis and strength.

ABCDEFGHIJKL
MNOPQRSTU
VWXYZ&

abcdefghijklmn
opqrstuvwxyz
1234567890

FUTURA LIGHT—A notable contribution to the sans-serif series
and which is especially useful where delicacy of effect is desired.

ABCDEFG
HIJKLMN
OPQRST
UVWXYZ

abcdefghijklmn
opqrstuvwxyz

ALBERTUS has a distinct character of its own and in its conformation
it is not unlike Gill.

27

ABCDEFGHIJK

LMNOPQRST

UVWXYZ&

GOTHIC CONDENSED—A letter of a very striking design in the
sans-serif class. As with all condensed types, this can be used where
economy of space is necessary.

abcdefghijkl
mnopqrstuv
wxyz

1234567890

ABCDEFG
HIJKLMN
OPQRSTU
VWXYZ

ELONGATED ROMAN SHADED

ABCDEFG
HIJKLMN
OPQRSTU
VWXYZ

SANS SERIF SHADED—An elongated style with legibility and
distinction.

ABCDE
FGHIJK
LMNOPV
QRSTU
WXYZ
1234567
890

GILL SHADOW—The shadow effect here gives a sense of considerable depth.

ROCKWELL SHADOW—A sturdy letter that looks effective in either one or two colours.

A B C D E
F G H I J
K L M N
O P Q R
S T U V
W X Y Z

A Roman letter with an unusual shading effect.

ABCDEFG
HIJKLMN
OPQRSTU
VWXYZ&

abcdefghijklmnopqrstu
vwxyz

1234567890

BERNHARD CURSIVE BOLD—There is much grace in the form of
this modern script.

A B C D E
F G H I J
K L M N O
P Q R S T
U V V W
W X Y Z

abcdefghijklmn
oppqrrstuvwxy

PEN SCRIPT, as this style is known, is one of the oldest forms
of script and remains in everyday use.

ABCDEFG
HIJKLMN
OPQRSTU
VWXYZ

abcdefghijklm
nopqrstuvwxyz

TRAFTON—A one-stroke letter dependent for its beauty on the even flow of the letters. A valuable time-saver and favourite for hand-written price tickets and showcards.

ABCDEFG
HIJKLMN
OPQRSTUV
WXYZ&

abcd
efghi
jklm

nopq
rstuv
wxyz

INFORMAL SCRIPT—Should be used sparingly as captions and not as straight copy. The light face is suitable for advertising cosmetics and the like. Where ruggedness is required it can be drawn in a bold face using a large pen.

A B C D E
F G H I J K
L M N O P
Q R S T U
V W X Y Z

This elegant yet legible style can be utilized for initials in many styles of lettering, both upright and sloping, and for the body matter in illuminated addresses, testimonials, etc.

ABCDEFG
HIJKLMN
OPQRSTU
VWXYZ

abcdefghi
jklmnopqr
stuvwxyz

An alphabet resembling 'Signal'. Heavy condensed scripts produce here and there areas of inarticulate darkness which reduce legibility. These have to be eliminated by tricks, slight falsities to the true rhythm to the style.

New Season's Displays The Scotchman

—Fastest Time Ever!

Old French Porcelain

A New Airline...

Yachting Club

Express When a jazz man's blue...

New World Exhibitions

Good Food News The largest range

A new Overseas Journal

United States Lines

Script lettering can speak with a variety of intonation—sometimes elegant,
or exciting; perhaps regal or racy.

Masculine

Script for Style

Parchment

Sophisticated

Ball-pointed

PEN APPLICATION

Moist *Feminine*

or dry

or both

Texture

Very Informal *Textile*

Calligraphy

BRUSH APPLICATION

the DEGREE of and the Quality

exaggeration

Possible

in Advertising script is determined by the structure

Varieties of script showing its endless possibilities.

of the letters—
especially
of the first letters
of the letters
AND
and by the Message
or
and by the words
of the WORD words
that must be
written

OLD ENGLISH—This straight-sided angular Gothic letter was the original style used for the printed page. There are, of course, many different interpretations in present-day use, but the basic forms remain the same. Hair lines for embellishment should be avoided since they detract from legibility.

abcde
fghijk
lmnop
qrstu
vwxyz

OLD ENGLISH LOWER CASE

1 2 3
4 5 6 7 8 9 0

CONDENSED SANS SERIF

---

1 2 3
4 5 6 7 8 9 0

GILL SANS BOLD CONDENSED

---

1 2 3
4 5 6 7 8 9 0

TRAFTON

1 2 3
4 5 6 7 8 9 0

Free and easy style for
script lettering

1 2 3
4 5 6 7 8 9 0

PERPETUA

1 2 3
4 5 6 7 8 9 0

GILL SANS MEDIUM ITALIC

ABCDEFGHIJKLM
NOPQRSTUVWXYZ

CENTURY

abcdefghijklm
nopqrstuvwxyz

1234567889

PLAYBILL—This dates from the days of the theatre poster and makes a heavy impact with its slab-like serifs and the emphasis on the horizontal strokes, which is in contrast to almost every other letter-form. Still surprisingly popular, it is an effective display face.

A B C D E F G

H I J K L M N

O P Q R S T U

V W X Y Z

a b c d e f g h

i j k l m n o p q

r s t u v w x y z

1 2 3 4 5 6 7 8 9

STUDIO—Based on the Amsterdam Type Foundry's design, this is a modern
one-stroke alphabet, especially suitable for showcard work.

ABCDEFGHIJ KLMNOPQRS TUVWXYZ&

abcdefghijklm nopqrstuvwxyz

1234567890

METROPOLIS—A modern heavy letter, almost in the spirit of Ultra
Bodoni, but free in its style.

A B C D E F G
H I J K L M N
O P Q R S T U
V W X Y Z

a b c d e f g h i j k
l m n o p q r s t u v
w x y z

1 2 3 4 5 6 7 8 9 0

An italic slab-serif letter, based on Ludlow Karnak heavy italic (by courtesy of Odhams Press). This style of heavy squat letter is much favoured for exhibition signs and shop fascia board work.

STENCIL based on the actual form of letters stencilled on packing cases—gives a note of the unusual.

ABCDEFGHI
JKLMNOPQR
STUVWXY & Z

abcdefghijklm
nopqrs_tuvwx
4 and 3 /

MODERN THICK AND THIN—The letter height is twice
as thick as the average width.

ABCDEF
GHIJKLM
MOPQRS
TUVWXY
Z&
123456789

Adapted from the well-known printer's type 'Cooper Black.' A speedy
bold alphabet for poster and showcard work.

abcdefgh
ijklmnop
qrstuvwx
yz

The lower case of the alphabet opposite. The style combines maximum boldness with clear-cut lines and complete legibility.

ABCDEF
GHIJKL
MNOPQ
RSTUV
WXYZ

Another modern thick and thin sans-serif, which is extremely well designed,
derived from Crous Vidal's 'Paris' typeface. This italic version has many
possible variations and weight.

ABCDEF
GHIJKL
MNOPQ
RSTUVW
XYZ abcdefghijk
lmnopqrstuvwxyz !_?

MODERN FRENCH for work requiring a light letter of simplicity
and a touch of exclusiveness.

ABCDEFGHIJ
KLMNOPQRS
TUVWXYZ

abcdefghijklm
nopqrstuvwxyz

1234567890

An example of a brush script lettering based on ATF's 'Dom Casual',
designed by Peter Dom.

ABCDEF
GHIJKLM
NOPQRST
UVWXYZ

abcdefghij
klmnopqrst
uvwxyz&!?

EASTERN—An alphabet designed on Oriental characters, principally the wedge in the crescent. There are obvious occasions for its use and it is quickly written.

61

ABCDE
FGHIJK
LMNOP
QRSTU
VWXYZ

CHRISTMAS—An example of how a season atmosphere can be introduced into the letter.